WEST HAM UNITED

Sarah Blackmore

D1584575

Published in association with The Basic Skills Agency

Hodder & Stoughton

A MEMBER OF THE HODDER HEADLINE GROUP

Acknowledgements

Cover: David Jacobs/Action Images.

*Photos: p. 27 © Action Images; p. 24 © Action-Plus; pp. 3, 21 © Allsport;
pp. 12, 18 Allsport Historical Collection © Hulton Deutsch; pp. 6, 15 © Hulton Getty.*

Orders: please contact Bookpoint Ltd, 130 Milton Park, Abingdon, Oxon OX14 4SB. Telephone: (44) 01235 400414. Fax: (44) 01235 400454. Lines are open from 9.00–6.00, Monday to Saturday, with a 24 hour message answering service. Email address: orders@bookpoint.co.uk

British Library Cataloguing in Publication Data
A catalogue record for this title is available from The British Library

ISBN 0 340 74740 4

First published 1999
Impression number   10 9 8 7 6 5 4 3 2
Year   2004 2003 2002 2001

Typeset by Fakenham Photosetting Ltd, Fakenham, Norfolk.
Printed in Great Britain for Hodder & Stoughton Educational, a division of Hodder Headline Plc, 338 Euston Road, London NW1 3BH by The Bath Press, Bath

Contents

1 From the Irons to the Hammers

West Ham United.
We know them as the Hammers.
We watch them at Upton Park.

The Hammers are in the Premier League.
It was not always so.

Upton Park was once a cabbage patch.
No one knew the Hammers.
The cheers were for
a team with a different name,
'The Irons'.

Let's go back.
Back to 1895.
Over one hundred years ago.

Back to Thames Ironworks.
It was a famous ship-building yard.

Thames Ironworks had a football team.
They were called Thames Ironworks FC.
They were known as the Irons.

Five years later in 1900,
the Irons were on the way up.
They moved into the Southern League.

The Irons then changed their name.
They turned professional.
They were no longer Thames Ironworks FC.
They were West Ham United FC.

The Hammers were on their way.

Upton Park, home of West Ham United.

The Hammers played in the Southern League.
They played well.

In 1904 the Boleyn Ground opened.
The Hammers moved
to the Boleyn Ground at Upton Park.

After the First World War,
the Hammers moved again.
This time into the Second Division.
In the 1922–23 season
they were runners up in Division Two.

2 The White Horse Final

Who has not heard of the FA Cup?
It is one of the greatest prizes.
All teams dream of winning.
All fans dream of seeing their team at Wembley.

Wembley!
One of the most famous grounds in the world.
Cup finals and Wembley go together.

The first Wembley final was in 1923.
The first ever Wembley Cup Final.
Who played?
West Ham of course.
West Ham v Bolton.

What a match!
It is a legend.
It is known as the 'White Horse Final'.

The white horse helped to control
the crowds at the first FA Cup Final
at Wembley, 28 April 1923.

The year was 1923.
The date was 28 April.
It was a fine spring day.
King George the Fifth was at Wembley.

Wembley could hold about 125,000 people.
It was thought to be big enough.
Big enough for a Cup Final.

But West Ham were playing.
The East End came to watch.
There were so many fans.

There were too many fans.
There were more than Wembley could hold.
Many more.

In fact there were about 250,000.
They all tried to get in.

It was too many.
The crowd was too big.
What happened?

The fans were well behaved.
The police did a good job.
The 'White Horse' was a police horse.

The white horse was called Billy.
It was ridden by Constable George Scorey.
He led the police.
This is why the match was called
'The White Horse Final'.

There were so many people trying to get in.
The match started late.
It was almost an hour late.

At last.
The game started.
The King watched.
The huge crowd watched.

All watched the Hammers' net.
The ball came close.
GOAL!

The first one.
1–0 to Bolton.

The Hammers were one down.
It was only the first half.

The second half.
The second goal.
Bolton were two up!

It was a lucky goal.
It was a rebound.

Some thought it came off the post.
But the ball had hit the crowd.
They were standing so near to the net!

FA Cup Final, 1923.
Final score at full time.
Bolton Wanderers 2 – West Ham United 0.

The Hammers did not win the cup.
But they showed that they could pull a crowd.
And what a crowd!

3 Hammers at Wembley

The White Horse Final
was the Hammers' first visit to Wembley.
It was not their last.

Back to 1940.
The Hammers faced Blackburn Rovers.
It was the Football League War Time Cup.

This time the cup went back to Upton Park.
West Ham beat Blackburn 1–0.

Three times the Hammers have taken the cup.
In 1964, 1975 and 1980
the Hammers won the FA Cup.

Each time the fans went mad.
They shouted.
They sang.

'I'm forever blowing bubbles'.
That's the fans' song at the Boleyn Ground.
They sang it at Wembley too.

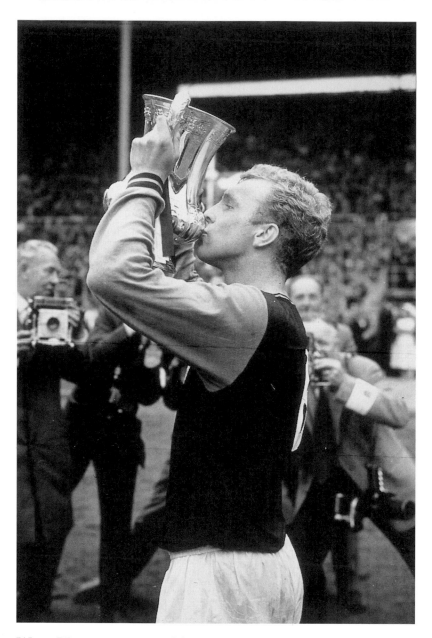

West Ham captain Bobby Moore
kisses the FA Cup
after beating Preston in the final.

12

The 1965 European Cup Winners Cup.
Again West Ham went to Wembley.
Again Wembley saw the Hammers win.

West Ham v TSV Munich.
The match was watched on TV by millions.
It was watched all over Europe.

It was a good game.
It is said to be one of the best.

The match was fast.
The teams were well matched.

Two goals.
In two minutes!

The scorer was Sealey.
The Hammers' reserve winger.
He made sure that the cup went to West Ham.

In 1981 the Hammers were back at Wembley.
It was the League Cup Final.
West Ham v Liverpool.

It had been a good season for West Ham.
They played in
the European Cup Winners Cup quarter finals.
They were top of the second division.

The Hammers' bid for trophies went on.
In 1989 the team were in the semi-final
of the Littlewood's Cup.
The next season they played in
the FA Cup semi-final.

In 1993 West Ham went up to the Premier League.

Sealey scores his first goal of the night
against TSV Munich in 1965.

4 Forever Hammers

'Who put the ball in the West Ham net?
Skip to my Lou Macari.'

This was the chant of
Manchester United fans at Old Trafford.

West Ham v Manchester United in 1973.
Macari scored the first goal.
In 1973 Lou Macari was
one of Manchester United's top players.

But 16 years later
Lou skipped again.
He skipped all the way to Upton Park.
He was the Hammers' sixth manager.

Hammer's managers so far have been

1902–1932	Syd King
1932–1950	Charlie Paynter
1950–1961	Ted Fenton
1961–1974	Ron Greenwood
1974–1989	John Lyall
1989–1990	Lou Macari
1990–1994	Billy Bonds
1994–2001	Harry Redknapp
2001–	Glenn Roeder

Billy Bonds was more than a manager.
He holds a club record.
He is the player with the most appearances.
His record stands at 663 league games.
132 cup games.

Billy was also in the Royal Honours List in 1998.
But he was not the only Hammer.
Also in the Honours were Bobby Moore
and Geoff Hurst,
Martin Peters
and Trevor Brooking.

Each one his own legend.

Billy Bonds holds the record
for most appearances in league games
for West Ham.

18

5 The Hammers who won the World Cup?

1966.
England v West Germany.
The World Cup.
Football's greatest prize.

Many say it was the best
English squad ever.
The only England team to win.
The best of the best.
And three of them were Hammers.

It was a record.
Only one English club
had three players in that team.

Bobby Moore was captain.
Geoff Hurst scored three goals.
Martin Peters scored one.

What club can boast more?

West Ham can.
Not only did Hammers play
in that famous match.
But they used a Hammers' free kick.

It was a free kick to the near post.
West Ham had worked on it a lot
at Upton Park.

They were experts at it.
It was this shot that got the equaliser
against West Germany.
The free kick got England back into the game.
They were losing 0–1 to West Germany.

Bobby Moore took the kick.
He curled the ball over to Geoff Hurst.
Hurst jumped to meet it.
He flicked it on.
And goal!
England were back level 1–1!

They went on to win 4–2.

West Ham's Geoff Hurst scored three goals
to help England win the 1966 World Cup.

21

6 Spotlight

We all have a Hammer we like the best.
He may be from the past.
He may be a more recent player.
He may be playing today.

Who do you think
is the greatest Hammer of all time?

Martin Peters, Geoff Hurst
or England captain Bobby Moore?
Trevor Brooking or Jimmy Greaves?
Pop Robson or Paul Ince?
Rio Ferdinand, Ian Bishop or Joe Cole?

It's hard to choose.
There have been so many great West Ham players.

7 I'm Forever Blowing Bubbles

Some of the best West Ham players
have been famous managers:
Malcolm Allison (Manchester City)
Dave Sexton (Chelsea)
Frank O'Farrell (Manchester United)
Noel Cantwell (Peterborough)
John Bond (Norwich City)

West Ham have only had 9 managers in 100 years.
They don't like change at West Ham.
But they know how to pick good managers:
Ron Greenwood,
John Lyall,
Billy Bonds,
Harry Redknapp.

Harry built a brilliant young team,
Some people think
it was best Hammers team since the 1960s.
Some people think
it was the best Hammers team ever.

Ian Bishop, whose passing skills
have set up many goals for West Ham.

24

West Ham had to sell some of their stars
and in 2001 Harry left the club.

But new manager Glenn Roeder still has some
top-class players.

Brilliant young midfielders like
Joe Cole and Michael Carrick.

Strong defenders like
Igor Stimac
and Nigel Winterburn

Dazzling forwards like
Paulo di Canio
and Freddie Kanoute.

Like all good West Ham teams
they don't always win.
But like all good West Ham teams
they always play good football.

There are more brilliant players on the way.
In 1999 West Ham won the FA Youth Cup.

The Hammers are improving the Boleyn Ground.
They want the stadium to be as good as the team.
It will soon hold 40,000 people.
Just think of 40,000 fans singing
the old Hammers' song:

'I'm forever blowing bubbles,
Pretty bubbles in the air,
They fly so high, nearly touch the sky,
Then like my dreams they fade and die.'

One thing is certain.
With Glenn Roeder's brilliant young players,
West Ham's dreams won't fade and die.

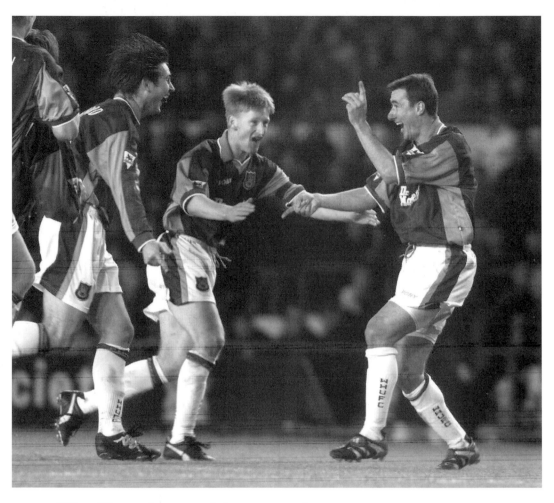

West Ham players celebrate a goal
against Derby County in the Premier League.

Record of Major Wins

Year	Team	Score	Competition
1903	Chatham	5–0	FA Cup
1914	Chesterfield	8–1	FA Cup
1923	Leicester	6–0	FA Cup
1958	Rotherham	8–0	League
1962	Manchester City	6–1	League
1966	Cardiff	5–1	League Cup
1967	Walsall	5–1	League Cup
1968	Sunderland	8–0	League
1983	Bury	10–0	League Cup

Record of Major Defeats

Year	Team	Score	Competition
1919	Barnsley	0–7	League
1927	Everton	0–7	League
1951	Sheffield Wednesday	0–6	League
1959	Sheffield Wednesday	0–7	League
1960	Huddersfield	1–5	FA Cup
1963	Blackburn	2–8	League
1978	QPR	1–6	FA Cup
1987	Barnsley	2–5	League Cup
1990	Oldham	0–6	League Cup